G-Rated Sex...

It's Really a God Thing

Dr. Jermone Glenn

Take note that the name satan and related names are not capitalized. We choose not to acknowledge him, even to the point of violating grammatical rules.

Revolution Publishing
25 S. Division Ave. Suite 525, Grand Rapids, MI 49503

For Worldwide Distribution Printed in the U.S.A.

This book and all other Revolution Publishing House books are available online at
www.jermoneglenn.com

TABLE OF CONTENTS

Sex is God's Idea

The media can't get enough of it. The lyrics in the music we hear are filled with it. Movies are talking about it. Magazines want to give you tips about it. It's the secret obsession of our society. The popular romance novel *50 Shades of Grey* by E.L. James revealed once again how profitable sex is. The majority of consumers for this book were women over 30. The series alone has sold over 100 million copies worldwide and the movie has made over $500 million worldwide!

Sexuality is exposed and available everywhere. Pornography is a multi-billion dollar industry. You no longer have to purchase it or go out of your home to get it. There is 24-hour access online at any time. Any person, child or adult, can see it with a computer or smartphone and an Internet connection at any point in the day. It's easier now than it has ever been to access pornography in secret.

Everyday we are bombarded with messages about sex. There is always someone that has an opinion about how to do it, when to do it, where to do it, and who to do it with. Sex before marriage has become so normal that the world questions your sexuality if you aren't promiscuous. Today there are more people having sex and less people falling in love, because when sex became easier to get, love became harder to find. Finding love use to take more effort and intentionality. People enjoyed spending the time to court someone. Now, it is more common for people to have sex before falling in love, when sex is supposed to be an expression of love.

With all these opinions about sex, it's hard to determine what is true and what is right. The truth is, sex came from God. It is a God thing. Genesis 2:24 says, "This is why a man leaves his father and mother and is united to his wife, and they become one flesh." (NIV). God established sex for man and woman to unite and become one.

The truth is, sex came from God. It is a God thing.

In this book, we won't just talk about not having sex, but we will talk about how to do it. We will talk about how to properly express your sexuality and how to recover from past hurts caused by misplaced sexuality.

Even though sex can be uncomfortable to talk about, it is important that you are completely honest with yourself while reading this book. There may be things in your past that left you ashamed and hurt. Up until now, you may not have wanted to talk about it, or even think about it. It may be painful, but after the pain comes healing. There will be healing in the end that will allow you to have a healthy sex life.

I encourage you to use this book as a journal. Pray with me at the end of each chapter and answer the reflection questions. Use the notes section to jot down your thoughts, prayers, feelings, and plans for the future. This book will help you begin to implement change and you will probably do more contemplating, reflecting, and planning than reading. If you put in the work, God will help you to overcome your insecurities, temptations, and past failures.

Even though the world has perverted sex,

it's important to remember that sex is God's

idea. It is a beautiful thing. We have gotten to a

point where people, particularly in the body of

Christ, feel uncomfortable discussing it, but if

everyone else can talk about it, we can too. It

doesn't belong to the world. The devil wants to

take it and keep us silent

If you put in the work, God will help you to overcome your insecurities, temptations, and past failures. about it, but it's time that

we take it back. You don't

have to be uncomfortable

talking about what God

created in the context He created it in. He

created it for a purpose.

Sex doesn't have to be a bad thing and you don't have to feel guilty about it. When you recognize the way God intended it, and have it in its proper context, you will see that it is beautiful and fulfilling and you will understand why God created it.

~ ~ ~

In order for us to understand God's view of sex, we must first acknowledge our own personal feelings about it. When you think about sex, how does it make you feel? Think of the time when you first learned about sex and where you hear about it the most. For many people, their beliefs about sex have been shaped by outside influences. When we formulate a belief system about something, it is

revealed in our behaviors.

People believe all kinds of things about sex

and most of them are misconceptions. When it

comes to what the Bible has to say about it,

many people think that it is outdated and

doesn't apply to us today, especially

considering how many people in the Bible have

had it outside of marriage and lived, such as

David and Abraham. They underestimate the

consequences because they are unaware of

what will happen when they do have sex or

they assume that the same thing that

happened to someone else will happen to

them. They believe that they know what to

expect, based on what happened to someone

else, but every story is different. What

happened, or didn't happen, to one person

may or may not happen with the next person.

For instance, just because a friend of yours

didn't get pregnant, doesn't mean you won't

either. They believe since they've seen certain

consequences, they can handle the outcome,

so what the Bible says doesn't apply to them,

but what God says about sex is still as true and

relevant today as it was in the Bible.

Another misconception that people believe is that premarital sex produces intimacy. "If I sleep with them, they'll stay with me," or "Sex will produce the love I'm not feeling." Sex is an expression of love, not a form of it. It deepens love that is already present. It is the add-on that further expresses what has already been established. Sex isn't strong enough to produce love on its own. There are

What God says about sex is still as true and relevant today as it was in the Bible.

many people who can have sex without having any emotions attached to it. With the popularity of one-night stands, sex has become a selfish, emotionless, strictly physical act. Once the

orgasm is done, so are the participants. There is

no foreplay, no intimacy, no sacredness, just

sex, and when you have sex looking for

intimacy that isn't there, it leaves you wanting

more rather than being fulfilled.

A third myth that people believe is that sex

is going to tell them if they're compatible with

Sex is an expression of love...it deepens love that is already present. the other person. They go
on a "test drive" to see if
they're compatible sexually.
You may have heard the

expression, "You have to test drive the car

before you buy it". This may be necessary when

buying an actual car, but it isn't necessary when

having sex.

A part of having sex with your spouse is

learning what their likes and dislikes are and

then it gets better the more you have it

together. You learn what their desires are and

seek to satisfy them and they do the same for

you in return. Through this learning process, your compatibility and chemistry gets deeper and you have better sex over time.

A part of having sex with your spouse is learning what their likes and dislikes are.

All these myths have been created from

outside influences and they have shaped a

belief system contrary to what God has for us. If our belief system of sex is influenced by the media, movies, and magazines, then we'll diminish the value of sex, but if we understand and believe what God says about sex, we will hold it in a higher regard.

In church, we generally don't talk about sex. Most churches don't talk about it at all. The ones that do try to educate people on God's rules about it. We hear, "Don't do it" or "You will get an STD if you do it unprotected," but we aren't given much information beyond that. We talk about what *not* to do more than we talk about what to do. There's always a fear associated with it. It's rare that we go in depth about sex and it has cultivated a culture of people that are uncomfortable talking about it, whether because of privacy, bad experiences, or being introduced to it in the wrong way. It seems off limits to talk about what to do and how to do it, even in the marriage context.

Sex isn't a dirty word. God *wants* you to have sex if you're married. Unfortunately, some people have only experienced sex in a way that leaves them feeling guilty and shameful. The devil has perverted it so much that some people feel guilty having sex even though they're married!

The truth is, God designed it to be an enjoyable experience, not an uncomfortable one. In fact, everyone who is married should be having sex. God wants us to be comfortable in our sexuality because He wants us to enjoy it and experience it with our spouses. He designed it to be pleasurable to both the husband and wife as they satisfy each other.

Sex is so intimate that it is a form of worship.

Sex is both powerful and passionate. It is a form and expression of love. Sex is so intimate that it is a form of worship. This is why it is so easy for people to fall into the habit of worshipping sex. While sex is supposed to be used as a tool for intimacy, it is often treated as a god by those who use it incorrectly. They let sex use them rather than using it.

In the Old Testament, within the Holy place of the tabernacle was a room called the Holy of Holies. A curtain, or veil, separated the Holy Place from the Holy of Holies. Whoever entered the Holy of Holies was coming into the literal presence of God. It was so intense that the High Priest was the only person allowed into this space and he was only allowed to go once a year and when he entered, he had to undergo a sanctification process. Anyone else who entered was to be put to death.

It was a serious instruction that wasn't to be taken lightly. The presence of God was incredibly powerful. Christ came to break this

shielded presence of God so all believers can

experience Him. This is essential in

understanding sex because Christ's relationship

with the church is synonymous to the

relationship between a husband and wife.

When we are in relationship with Christ, we are

able to go "beyond the veil" and experience

God's presence. When a man and woman get

married, they are then able to go "beyond the

Lovemaking is the highest expression of human ecstasy on Earth.

veil" in their relationship to

this deeply intimate place. It

is the only time a man and

woman are physically

inseparable. They are no longer two, but become one unit, not just in spirit, but also in flesh. The act in itself brings both of them to a place of oneness.

Lovemaking is the highest expression of human ecstasy on Earth. That moment of climax is such a vulnerable place. This is why it should not be shared with just anybody. Both people are left vulnerable, naked, and weak in that moment. This is the way God intended it. Sex can bring a marriage couple closer together, but with all the power it holds, it can be dangerous to those who aren't married.

My Prayer for You:

Father I pray in the name of Jesus that you reach and solidify every heart and bring us to a higher level of consciousness. Let out behaviors match our minds. We've been misinformed and ill-informed by the enemy about what sex is and we've taken it out of context, but you have laid out in Your Word a real plan for how You want it to be explored and experienced. Take the dirty away from it. Take the nasty off of it. Take the discomfort from it. Heal the brokenness and the wounds that this Word brings. Heal the places of molestation, fornication, and adultery that the Word brings. Heal the hurt places and the broken places that the Word brings. Bring about healing, God, so people will walk in transformation and they will be ready for the next dimension that you have for us to live and to walk in.

We honor the marriage bed. It is sacred. It is holy. It is a place where You desire for us to explore and experience our highest level of intimacy that two people can experience on Earth, the place where we become one. The enemy is a lie. He has no place and no power. I pray that no one has deaf ears and the conviction power of the Holy Spirit will grapple the hearts of those of us who have been married and committed adultery, those who are in adulterous relationships, those who aren't married and are fornicating, and those of

us who are married that are holding back, not

exploring the fullness of what you have for us

for control and manipulation. I break the power

of the enemy today in Jesus' name. Amen.

Reflection:

How did you first learn about sex?

_____

_____

_____

Where do you get your information about sex?

_____

_____

_____

How has this affected your behaviors?

_____

_____

_____

Notes:

_____

_____

_____

_____

_____

_____

_____

_____

_____

_____

_____

_____

_____

Everybody Should be Having Sex...if They are Married

[1]Now for the matters you wrote about: "It is good for a man not to have sexual relations with a woman." [2]But since sexual immorality is occurring, each man should have sexual relations with his own wife, and each woman with her own husband. [3]The husband should fulfill his marital duty to his wife, and likewise the wife to her husband. [4]The wife does not have authority over her own body but yields it to her husband. In the same way, the husband does

not have authority over his own body but yields it to his wife. [5]Do not deprive each other except perhaps by mutual consent and for a time, so that you may devote yourselves to prayer. Then come together again so that Satan will not tempt you because of your lack of self-control. [6]I say this as a concession, not as a command. [7]I wish that all of you were as I am. But each of you has your own gift from God; one has this gift, another has that.

1 Corinthians 7:1-9, NIV

What is so bad about having sex outside of marriage? Society likes to tell us that there is nothing wrong with it. Let's think of sex like a fire. Fire is beautiful in the fireplace. It keeps you warm. It's a beautiful thing to look at, and in the fireplace, it serves a great purpose, but if that same fire gets somewhere else in your house, it'll burn whatever it comes in contact with. Sex is the same way. It is safe and beautiful in the confines of marriage, but outside a marriage, it will start burning whatever it comes in contact with, setting it on fire, leaving you to wonder what happened.

God draws a firm line against casual and illicit sex (Hebrews 11:4). He does this because He knows there are so many consequences connected to it. The bottom line is, sex is for marriage. Sex outside of marriage holds too many restraints. God knows how powerful sex is so He tries to protect us from the outcomes that come from having it outside the safety of marriage. You already know about the dangers of unplanned pregnancy and STDs, but there are many other consequences that tend to fall under the radar:

Sex is for marriage. Sex outside of marriage holds too many restraints.

There is no safety and no confidentiality. There are many ties, fears, and insecurities with sex outside of marriage. Without a covenant relationship, there is no security. When two people have sex outside of marriage, they end up having to ask each other a lot of questions that they don't have to ask with a spouse: "How many partners have you had?" "Do you have a condom?" "Do you have an STD?" "Did you get tested? When?" After seeing each other naked and having a very intimate moment, both are left in a vulnerable and empty place.

Having sex distorts your thinking. This
is supposed to happen because sex is intended
to bring you into a deeper place with your
spouse, but outside of marriage, it is
dangerous. Many people have compromised
their values and lowered their standards after
having sex. Things that they would normally
say no to, they begin to accept and things that

*Many people have
compromised their
values and lowered
their standards
after having sex.*
used to be deal
breakers for them are
now things they
tolerate.

**Having premarital sex will affect how
you approach sex with your spouse when**

you do get married. This is a particularly unfortunate thing because it affects the person you want to spend the rest of your life with the most. For most people, this is unintentional, but they end up bringing past memories into the marriage bed. Many people don't realize it, and some try to hide it, but the truth is, exploring sex outside of marriage has an effect on the sex a person has with their spouse when they do get married.

The spouse ends up competing with someone else and they may wonder, "Are they making love to me or to someone else in their mind?" The more someone has sex outside of marriage, the harder it will be to be completely intimate with their spouse when they do get

married.

The more someone has sex outside of marriage, the harder it will be to be completely intimate with their spouse when they do get married.

If you find yourself in this situation, God can help you to recover from the insecurities of your past because without God, it is impossible to have endless sexual encounters and come to the marriage bed and feel whole. If you're willing to go through the process, He can help you to get rid of all the baggage. Sex can be sacred and brand new without tainting it by mentally comparing them to previous experiences.

You develop soul ties. The term "soul tie" is not in the Bible. It is a term used to describe the reality of two souls connecting and becoming one. We get our emotions, passions, desires, appetites, and feelings at the seat of our soul so a close relationship can feel like a soul tie, but having a close relationship based on personality and mutual love doesn't mean the two souls are intertwined.

God created us to have this deep level of bonding so it's natural to desire deep connections with other people. We are created to be "joined" or "knit together" and become what the Bible calls "one flesh." One flesh means to have sexual intercourse on the physical level and to enjoy a mystic

communion on the spiritual level.

When you have sex, your two souls

become one and you are bound to that person

in a spiritual way. This can be beautiful in

One flesh means marriage, but a real
to have sexual
intercourse on the problem outside of it. In
physical level and God's eyes, sex is an act
to enjoy a mystic
communion on the of marriage through
spiritual level. consummation, meaning

that every time an unmarried person has sex,

they become married to the person they've had

sex with.

It's difficult to break soul ties, especially

without God's help because of how deeply you

become connected to the other person. God

forbids it because it is harmful. If you have any

unhealthy soul ties, it is

best to break them

before you get married.

If you want to know

more about soul ties, I

suggest reading

Every time an unmarried person has sex, they become married to the person they've had sex with.

Breaking Unhealthy Soul Ties by Bill and Sue

Banks. We will discuss steps on how to break

soul ties in the last chapter.

My Prayer for You:

You have prophesied, God. This is the season where the flesh wants to participate in the process. You have great plans laid out and the enemy is waiting to snatch us up, to trick us, and to get us involved in things that are not becoming to Your plan and Your will. Father I pray for a supernatural power to break and destroy every yoke that takes everything out of context as we learn, grow, live, and move. I pray in the name of Jesus that the life-changing power of the Holy Spirit will take control of our hearts and minds. Restore our virtue. Put it in proper perspective. Tear up the plans of the enemy. Erase and heal the memories in our minds, God. Bring restoration in Jesus' name.

Amen.

Reflection:

Do you think abstinence is unrealistic? Why?

_____

_____

_____

_____

If you have had sex before marriage, what kind

of impact has it had on your other

relationships?

_____

_____

_____

_____

_____

Do you still feel connected to that person, or those people that you were intimate with? If you do, you may have soul ties that need to be resolved.

_____

_____

Notes:

_____

_____

_____

_____

_____

_____

It's All About Your Body

¹² *Just because something is technically legal doesn't mean that it's spiritually appropriate. If I went around doing whatever I thought I could get by with, I'd be a slave to my whims.*

¹³ *You know the old saying, "First you eat to live, and then you live to eat"? Well, it may be true that the body is only a temporary thing, but that's no excuse for stuffing your body with food, or indulging it with sex. Since the Master honors you with a body, honor him with your body!*

¹⁴⁻¹⁵ *God honored the Master's body by raising it from the grave. He'll treat yours with the same*

resurrection power. Until that time, remember

that your bodies are created with the same

dignity as the Master's body. You wouldn't take

the Master's body off to a whorehouse, would

you? I should hope not.

16-20 There's more to sex than mere skin on skin.

Sex is as much spiritual mystery as physical fact.

As written in Scripture, "The two become one."

Since we want to become spiritually one with

the Master, we must not pursue the kind of sex

that avoids commitment and intimacy, leaving

us more lonely than ever—the kind of sex that

can never "become one." There is a sense in

which sexual sins are different from all others. In

sexual sin we violate the sacredness of our own

bodies, these bodies that were made for God-given and God-modeled love, for "becoming one" with another. Or didn't you realize that your body is a sacred place, the place of the Holy Spirit? Don't you see that you can't live however you please, squandering what God paid such a high price for? The physical part of you is not some piece of property belonging to the spiritual part of you. God owns the whole works. So let people see God in and through your body.

1 Corinthians 6:12-20

The wife does not have authority over her own body but yields it to her husband. In the same way, the husband does not have authority over his own body but yields it to his wife.

1 Corinthians 7:4, NIV

When you get married and have sex with your spouse, you are seeking to satisfy them, and they are seeking to satisfy you. To understand this better, we must understand the truth about our bodies. We like to take ownership over our own bodies, but the truth is, whether you're married or not, your body belongs to someone else. If you are married, it belongs to your spouse and if you are single, your body belongs to Christ. When you get married, you look how your spouse wants you to look because your bodies

If you are married, your body belongs to your spouse and if you are single, your body belongs to Christ.

belong to each other. It's not a controlling thing, but it's a mutual understanding between the two of you. You give the same concessions that you require in each other. You seek to please each other in what you wear, how you act, and how you look. You satisfy each other inside and outside the bedroom.

The marriage bed should be a place of mutuality: the woman seeking to satisfy her man and the man seeking to satisfy his woman. Men are stimulated by what they see. Women are stimulated by what they hear, making them feel safe, secure, protected, and respected. In pleasing your spouse, you both come into your sacred space ready for each other, such as putting on cologne, lighting candles, and wearing lingerie. You do what your spouse likes. This is a conversation that you have with each other, which we will discuss more in the next chapter. Don't assume that you automatically know what they want. Talk to each other about what you like and what you don't like. It's your place to develop confidence and chemistry. You have freedom in your bedroom. There are no boundaries inside the bedroom between a husband and wife. The only boundary God puts on sex is that you have to be married and it's free for you to enjoy with just each other.

There are no boundaries inside the bedroom between a husband and wife.

The devil's plan is to use sex against couples in their marriage. He wants to get you to withhold sex from your partner or use it for control and manipulation. This creates a space for the enemy to come in and use sex against you in all kinds of crafty ways because he knows what kind of bond comes with having sex. If you remember that your bodies belong to each other and consistently seek to please each other, you will not fall into this trap.

When you're single, your body belongs to the Lord. You're married to God. Your commitment, covenant, and time all belong to

Him. God owns the whole work: body, soul, and spirit. Your body is a temple: the very sanctuary of the Holy Spirit. Let people see the God in you. Your single life is your time to build your commitment to God. Learn to be faithful to God before you get married. If you're not able to be faithful to God before you get married, you will not be able to be faithful to your spouse when you do get married. Get in the habit of giving your body back to God every day, one day at a time.

Some of you may be asking, "If my sexuality is a God thing and He authorized it and gave it me, what do I do if I'm not in my season to explore it?" God says it shouldn't be expressed outside the marriage bed, but it's

understandable that you have real desires that

want to be expressed. These are real feelings

If you're not able to be faithful to God before you get married, you will not be able to be faithful to your spouse when you do get married.

that you have to deal with so

what do you do with it? To

explore this, let's take a look

at 1 Corinthians 6:9-11:

Don't you realize that this is not the way to live? Unjust people who don't care about God will not be joining in his kingdom. Those who use and abuse each other, use and abuse sex, use and abuse the earth and everything in it, don't qualify as citizens in God's kingdom. A number of you know from experience what I'm talking about, for not so long ago you were on that list. Since then, you've been cleaned up and given a fresh start by Jesus, our Master, our Messiah, and by our God present in us, the Spirit.

When you are a part of the kingdom of God, you live by a whole new standard. If you consider yourself a part of the kingdom, you have to live by the laws of the spirit as well as the laws of the flesh. Sometimes it's easier to do spiritual things, such as having faith and believing in God while it's more difficult to deny ourselves the desires of our flesh. It is a real battle, but God still has His principles that He wants us to live by.

Therefore, we can't base our lives on what the world is doing. We can't base our lives on people that aren't going where we're trying to go and doing what we're trying to do if they're living by a different moral code. We are a part of the kingdom and we live by that standard, whether it's the time for harvest and rewards or discipline and denial. We are participants when it comes to both matters of faith and matters of flesh.

We are participants when it comes to both matters of faith and matters of flesh.

What if you're facing these temptations and you're in a relationship with someone you're not married to yet? The best way to handle those feelings is to change your surroundings. Instead of spending so much time alone, hang out with friends, go on group dates, spend time together in public settings, and shift the focus of your conversations. Refrain from spending so much intimate time alone.

Before my wife and I got married, we spent a lot of time at her grandmother's house and my mom's house. We intentionally spent time in group gatherings to help us with the temptation. We also thought a lot about what we wanted to tell future leaders one day. We considered the story we wanted to tell our children. Would we want to say, "Oops, we messed up and God forgave us," or "We were able to abstain from sex and you can too." Think about what you would want to tell your future children someday. What would you want to tell a young person that looks up to you? You can do it if you set these boundaries.

If you are in this type of relationship, it's important that both people are dedicated to the commitment. If not, it may be time to end the relationship because your values are different and the relationship may not be healthy. This doesn't mean that one person won't have a weak moment. It does mean, however, that when one has a weak moment, the other one is strong enough to help them through it.

If the feelings are consistently becoming stronger and stronger no matter how hard you try to abstain, particularly for men, it may be a sign that it's time to take the relationship to the next level and get married. It's an indication, not that you just want sex, but that the relationship is ready to evolve and escalate. We usually like to take our flesh to the next level first, but it's best to take the relationship to the next level by creating a covenant through

marriage so the two of you can grow on a

spiritual and emotional level together first, then

seal it and enhance it with sex afterwards.

My Prayer for You:

Lord we accept Your forgiveness. We accept Your power to overcome. We are overcomers. I thank You for Your blood that washes and cleanses us. Lord, we give our bodies to You. We give You our desires. Change our appetites. Give us what You want from us. Give us the desires of Your heart. Father, we raise our standards. Heal us from the past as we walk into our futures. We will not be controlled by moods and whims. We have Your grace. We accept your Spirit. We accept what You did for us on Calvary. Thank You for giving us Your body. Now our bodies belong to You. Let them be a temple for You. Let them bring glory to You. Teach us how to live for You because we don't know how.

From this day forward, everyday we will make a conscious choice to give You our bodies. Satan, you have no more power over our lives. I renounce you. We resist you. I release you from any control in the lives of God's people. We belong to Jesus. He is our Lord. He is our Master. He is our Savior. We are forgiven, whole, free, and victorious. I cast down every thought that exalts itself against the knowledge of God. I thank you today, Lord, for saving, forgiving, and keeping us in Jesus' name. We'll get everything that belongs to us. Now have mercy on us and spare us from the consequences of our actions. We receive the

plan of God that's coming to our lives now.

Give us courage to do what you tell us to do in

Jesus' name. Amen.

Reflection (for those that are single):

What are some ways that you can change the way you handle your body so that it reflects Christ?

_____

_____

_____

If you don't have a spouse, you are married to Christ. What aspects of this type of relationship can best be improved on in your personal relationship with Him (ie. trust, love, faithfulness, quality time)?

_____

_____

Write down what steps you plan to take to

enhance those aspects.

_____

_____

_____

_____

_____

_____

_____

_____

_____

_____

_____

Notes:

Sex is Better When You Know How to Do It

Honor marriage, and guard the sacredness of sexual intimacy between wife and husband. God draws a firm line against casual and illicit sex.

Hebrews 13:4

Marriage should be honored by all, and the marriage bed kept pure, for God will judge the adulterer and all the sexually immoral.

Hebrews 13:4, NIV

It is clear from what you've already read so far that sex can be a complex thing. Before we go any further, I want you to understand a few things about sex:

- Sex is not love.

- Sex is not spiritual.

- Sex is 100 percent physical and chemical.

- Sex is for procreation.

- Sex is for recreation and release.

- Sex is for communication.

- Sex is a metaphor.

- Sex is for marriage.

You read earlier that sex is a form of worship. The husband and wife go "beyond the veil" into the inner courts of their relationship.

It's sacred. The two of them become one and

they come together in a deeper way than they

ever have before. They're one in the bedroom

and they still act like they are one outside the

bedroom. This means that when they're away

from each other, they still

The two of them act as if they're with each
become one and
they come other. They don't act like
together in a one in the bedroom and
deeper way than
ever before. single in public.

When you wait to have sex until you get

married, you leave yourself open and

vulnerable to your spouse in a healthy way. It

keeps things simple. You come to the marriage

with a clean slate. You have no one to compare them to sexually.

You have a clear heart and mind when going into the relationship. You read earlier that sex distorts your thinking. Good sex can make you compromise your values. Bad sex can make you overlook the good in a person. When you wait, you are in the relationship with a clear perspective. You are able to discern the future of the relationship, their capacity, and the potential for it to grow into something more. You are more at peace and you avoid all the problems that come with premarital sex.

Sex is a private, intimate moment that involves just the husband and wife. It isn't a news story to be discussed with friends, family, and social media. It's your place to serve your spouse privately. It's something that belongs to just the two of you. You become confident and chemically connected to the physical attraction that happens in your marriage bed.

It is a place of intimacy where you can share your deepest inhibitions and greatest fears with your spouse and nobody else. Sex in marriage is about pleasing each other, instead of being all about performance. You allow your partner to be sexually expressive with you in a way that they are comfortable.

Sex in marriage is about pleasing each other, instead of being all about performance.

There is a safety that comes with the covenant of marriage. You read in the last chapter that having sex distorts your thinking and it brings you into a deeper place with your spouse. In a covenant marriage, you don't have to worry about the decisions you make afterwards regarding your relationship because you have already decided to spend the rest of your life with them. You don't have to worry about lowering your standards because you already know your spouse and they have met your standards outside the bedroom. You don't have to worry about asking your spouse questions about their past or wondering if they will get up and leave once you've had sex. You are free to comfortably enjoy each other's presence after having sex, rather than feeling awkward about it. You are comfortable and protected in your nudity.

When you come into the marriage bed, you come without bringing your past experiences. You come with a fresh slate. We will talk about recovering from a sexual past in the "Sexual Healing" chapter.

You can get sexual healing before you get married, however, when you do get married, you must have conversations with your spouse about sex in order for the two of

you to have a healthy sex life.

Imagine that you've had a promiscuous

lifestyle, but you decide to leave it behind

when you meet the one

You must have
conversations
with your spouse
about sex in
order for the two
of you to have a
healthy sex life.

that you're going to

marry. The two of you

decide to wait to have sex

until you get married.

Your wedding night finally

arrives and both of you are excited. The room

is set and you're both gassed up to go. It's

perfect. You both make your way to the king

size bed in the middle of the room. Right as

you pull the covers off the perfectly made bed,

you see dozens of dirty, crumpled pieces of paper and as you read them, each contains sexual partners, experiences, and preferences accumulated from your past. Not very romantic, is it?

This is what happens when you bring past experiences into your marriage without healing from them and talking it through with your spouse. It's very easy to bring certain expectations into your marriage if you have experience with sex already. Some people bring their pride and ego into a marriage if they were good at sex and some bring shame if they were bad at it, while there are others that think they were better than they actually are.

Regardless of where you've been, the key is to start fresh. This will clean out your bed. The key to this is having a completely open and honest conversation with your spouse.

Have a sex interview with them. It will be exciting and you'll learn a lot. In these conversations, discuss your expectations in the bedroom. Discuss attire preferences. What do you want them to look like? Do you prefer

Have a sex interview with your spouse.

make-up or all natural? Are you okay with them having their pajamas on, looking like they are ready for bed or do you prefer them to maintain how they've looked throughout the day and get ready for bed later? Do you like to play dress up? Do you like lingerie or would you prefer to come into the room already naked and ready to go? Do you like costumes?

Discuss how you want the room to look. Do you like candles? Would you prefer the lights on or off? Figure out if they like foreplay and what types they like.

Consider what kinds of things you want to bring into the bedroom. It's okay to bring food, toys, props, and cameras (although I wouldn't recommend cameras) to the bedroom. Read books together and get other educational resources. Take a trip to the store and pick some things out that you and your spouse like together. It's your sex life. Have fun

and make the most of it. Explore it

wholeheartedly. There is no greater exploration

than your own experiences with each other.

It's your bed and your marriage. Do

what you want. People often wonder what's

permissible in the marriage bed. As long as it's

agreed upon by both parties, and it includes

just the two of you

(that means no *It's your sex life.*

Have fun and

threesomes) and *make the most* it's

not illegal, you can *of it.* do

whatever you want. Don't be ashamed of what

you like, no matter how outlandish it may

seem. You didn't get married to be prude and

82

uptight in bed. It should be exciting. It's an

exploration and a conversation. You come with

a clean slate without assuming that you know

what your spouse wants and not giving them

what any of your last partners wanted.

Don't be ashamed of what you like, no matter how outlandish it may seem

Be comfortable about your sexual expectations. Respect what your partner may or may not be comfortable with. Listen to what

their expectations are. Although the two of you

respect whatever boundaries and reservations

you have regarding sex, it's important that you

both also come to the marriage bed with an

open mind, willing to explore areas that you

may not have explored before or explore something you may not have liked in a past relationship. Just because you didn't like it with someone else doesn't mean that you won't like it with your spouse.

If you are married, have the interview. It is completely appropriate. In addition to what you like and dislike sexually, it's also important to discuss child planning. Do you want children? If you both agree to not have children at the moment, what birth control methods will you use? Some women do not like taking birth control because of the way it affects their body (hormonal changes, weight fluctuations, bloating, etc.). Because of this, some women want their husbands to wear condoms, but there are men out there who don't want to wear condoms when they get married. They may have been taught that condoms are for avoiding STDs. They believe they are reserved for women that you're not married to. This all can be flushed out with sex interviews with your spouse. Finding the balance is only going to come through conversation. You will be more comfortable with each other, you will come closer together, and have more fun while doing it.

My Prayer for You:

Father I pray virtue, value, restoration, and healing today over the lives of your people. I thank You for the words that have been spoken. Somebody needs to be saved and give their lives to You today. Somebody needs to be restored today. Whatever it is, you know and they know. Let their hearts be touched and transformed. Restore virtue and value. We break every stronghold, every ex that's still playing games. I pray in the name of Jesus, that you will shake it up, grab it out, and root it out so that wholeness can take place. We won't be condemned. We'll be convicted. There is therefore now no condemnation. We align ourselves to come into order with your

plan. Give us power over our flesh. Give us

discipline over our minds, Father. Let us make

better choices and not compromise. We

declare it. We decree it. We confess it. We say

yes. We open ourselves up to it. Deliver today.

Set free in the name of Jesus. Bring us into a

healthy perspective. Let us not ignore what

your Word says, but bring us to a healthy place,

in Jesus' name. Amen.

Reflection (for those that are married):

It's time to have some fun. Have the sex

interview with your husband or wife and write

down what their requests are. Then, the next

time you have sex, seek to please each other in

the manner you discussed.

Sexual Healing

1-2 Jesus went across to Mount Olives, but he was soon back in the Temple again. Swarms of people came to him. He sat down and taught them.

3-6 The religion scholars and Pharisees led in a woman who had been caught in an act of adultery. They stood her in plain sight of everyone and said, "Teacher, this woman was caught red-handed in the act of adultery. Moses, in the Law, gives orders to stone such persons. What do you say?" They were trying to trap him into saying something incriminating so they could bring charges against him.

6-8 *Jesus bent down and wrote with his finger in the dirt. They kept at him, badgering him. He straightened up and said, "The sinless one among you, go first: Throw the stone." Bending down again, he wrote some more in the dirt.*

9-10 *Hearing that, they walked away, one after another, beginning with the oldest. The woman was left alone. Jesus stood up and spoke to her. "Woman, where are they? Does no one condemn you?"*

11 *"No one, Master."*

"Neither do I," said Jesus. "Go on your way. From now on, don't sin."

John 8:1-11

Our sexual identity needs reshaping. Sex is a God thing and it cannot be fixed unless we are willing to admit it is broken. If we want to be in a healthy marriage relationship, we must come to terms with every sexual encounter and experience of the past or else we will drag baggage in the

Our sexual identity needs reshaping.

bedroom and share it with our spouses. What do you do when you find yourself in this type of situation where your values and virtue have been lost and compromised? Jesus found himself in a scenario in John 8, where this very thing happened to an adulterous woman.

Jesus was in the temple courts in front of all the people, ready to teach, when the teachers of the law came to interrupt Him because they caught a woman in adultery. They brought her to Jesus and said, "Jesus, this woman was caught in the act of adultery." The Law of Moses declared that they should stone her for what she did. The leaders were using the woman as a trap to trick Jesus, because if Jesus said she shouldn't be stoned, He would be accused of violating the law, but if He gave them permission to stone her, they could report Him to the Romans, who didn't allow the Jews to perform their own executions. They laid her at the feet of Jesus while everyone was watching to see what He was going to say.

Everybody in the crowd was looking to see

what Jesus was going to do to this woman.

93

Adultery and fornication don't cover you. They expose you.

Anytime you partake in infidelity or fornication, it leaves you open, exposed, and vulnerable. It leaves you in a place where you have to face the consequences of your actions. It puts you in a compromising situation. Marriage is supposed to protect you from being vulnerable to those outside situations. Adultery and fornication don't cover you. They expose you. It makes you vulnerable and open to other people. You become exposed when you are supposed to be covered and it always puts you in a situation where you have to come before Jesus. You may not realize it in the moment, because at that time, it's all about having fun, but every time you have sex with someone, you leave a piece of you with them. You break yourself and expose yourself all over again each time you get in bed with someone that isn't your spouse.

Some people use sex as a way to cover up deeper hurts and frustrations. They subconsciously believe it will bring healing, but it will never heal them. It exposes you, breaks you, and brings pain that can't be covered up. Sex outside of marriage provides a temporary fix for those involved, and most times, leaves them more broken than they would like to admit. So if you've been broken, how do you begin the healing process?

Expose the secrets. The truth is, you are only as sick as your secrets. Keeping secrets can cripple your spiritual growth and your relationship with God. Are there things you feel that you can't expose or talk about? If the answer is yes, you might still be living in secret. It doesn't mean you have to tell everybody all your business, but you at least have to be honest with yourself and with God.

You are only as sick as your secrets.

The adulterous woman's secret was put out in the open before Jesus. Jesus will use what others try and use against you and make it work for you if you are willing to be uncovered for Him. We spend more time trying to close the closet instead of cleaning out the closet. Cleaning it out allows Jesus to take care of it, because eventually the closet will open. You may have some stuff that you're not proud of, but take everything out one by one and put it in God's hands. When you reveal it to Him, He will keep it safe from others. Being completely honest with Him will open the way for you to be truly healed. He sees those things about you and still wants you and loves you. When you face it, you can walk with the boldness that's necessary to encounter your past.

After you are honest with yourself and Jesus, tell your spouse if you're married. If you can't trust anyone else, you should be able to

trust them. There are a lot of people who plan

a wedding, but not a marriage. They plan the

colors they'll wear, who's going to be in it, and

where it's going to be, but they don't plan for

the actual marriage and the problems of the

past end up creeping into the relationship.

There are no marriage problems. There are people with problems that get married.

Issues arise when people

with problems get married

and refuse to deal with

them. Their past explodes

in the marriage. Andy

Stanley once said, "There are no marriage

problems. There are people with problems that

get married." The fewer the secrets in a

marriage, the greater the success because

you're never worried about who will come

around and expose them to your spouse.

Find a friend who will let you confide

in them. Exposing your secrets to the right

people is healthy. Secrets destroy relationships,

but talking them through with the right people

brings healing.

Secrets destroy relationships, but talking them through with the right people brings healing.

Find a friend that lets you know when you're doing something wrong and it's time to get yourself together. This is a

real friend. Real friends do not hide your bad

habits, but they help you get over them. Real

friends will listen to your secrets and won't use them against you later. You need a friend that will pray and fast for you. If you know a friend needs help with something, help them. Find a real friend and be a real friend. Most people keep secrets because they don't have anyone to tell their secrets to. If you don't have a friend like that, pray for one. God will send one to you.

Sin no more. Although the crowd meant to do the woman harm by bringing her before everyone with her sin, it was good that they brought her to Jesus because if they never did, she would have been sneaking in the bedroom, still in her situation.

Sometimes Jesus will yank you out of your situation to expose it so you won't settle for less than you deserve. He wants to take you out of what is less than you. Sometimes we need to be dragged out of our mess, because we like it even though it is harmful to us. You may not like when He takes you out of it, but you will appreciate it later. Your potential, future, and power are too great for God to leave you where He found you. No matter what your struggle is, He will bring you out of it.

When God brings you out of your mess,

When God brings you out of your mess, He brings you out with no condemnation.

He brings you out with no condemnation. The

crowd wanted to condemn her but Jesus sent all of them away and He was the only one left who had the power to judge her. The law said she deserved to die. The only people that could condemn her were her husband and the priest. She wasn't married and the priests were not around. Jesus became her priest and her husband. He didn't give in to them trying to judge her. So although He could, He chose not to. Instead He told her to "go and sin no more" (John 8:11).

Even though God won't condemn you, He will correct you. Having no condemnation is not a license to sin. It is an opportunity to accept His forgiveness and make changes.

When Jesus told the woman to sin no more, it didn't mean she would never sin again. It meant that she should no longer be a part of that lifestyle. Like the adulterous woman, we also deserve death for our sins, but Jesus has let us live. No condemnation says, "I'm glad I got off, but I need to change." He wants us to leave that lifestyle as well and even if we mess up, He is there to forgive and correct us because we can't do it on our own. We need Him to help us out of it.

Resist Temptation. In our society, we try and teach our girls that they should hold their virtue, but this is something that we all should be doing, both men and women. When you hold your virtue, you have high value. It can be difficult to do so, especially in the modern day society we live in.

Many people are addicted to intensity, particularly when it comes to sex. Intensity comes from the risks you take: "We could get caught for this" or "We shouldn't be doing this." People worry about intensity and forget about intimacy because intimacy exposes you. You can have intimacy with your spouse if you're married and with God if you're single.

Intensity is a problem both inside and outside of marriages. We like to think that marriage will solve those temptations, but unfortunately, that is not the case. This is why there is infidelity in marriages. People think marriage is a cure for lust, but you can still be tempted with lust after marriage. Lust is a spirit and only God can cure it. If the spirit is in you, you still have to fight it when you get married. This is why it is best to develop this discipline in your single life. When people don't know how to say no, even though they are in a marriage, they never get enough.

When temptation comes, God always provides a way of escape. 1 Corinthians 10:13 says, *"No temptation has overtaken you that is not common to man. God is faithful, and he will not let you be tempted beyond your ability, but with the temptation he will also provide the way of escape, that you may be able to endure it"*

(ESV).

Temptation and escape are twins and they never show up without each other. You have a choice. It's an exercise of your will. Temptation never shows up with what you don't like. It always shows up just the way you like it. Aristotle said, "What lies in your power to do also lies in your power not to do." It's no doubt that you will be tempted, but you have the power to walk away from it.

Temptation and escape are twins and they never show up without each other.

Openly get rid of every impure thought. The Bible says that we don't war in

What lies in your power to do also lies in your power not to do.

the flesh. We fight in the spirit, "*Casting down imaginations, and every high thing that exalteth itself against the knowledge of God, and bringing into captivity every thought to the obedience of Christ;*" (2 Corinthians 10:5, KJV).

When you give into temptation, your flesh is fed and becomes a secret thing that grows in the dark. The secret sin that grows in the dark has power to control your life. The trick of the enemy is to keep it trapped and locked in your mind. The truth is, we can have some crazy thoughts. We have these thoughts and wonder where they come from. The devil will try to put impure thoughts in your brain to

get you to sin against God.

The best way to

The secret sin that grows in the dark has power to control your life.

combat this is to cast down

the thought as soon as it

enters your mind. You can't

fight a thought with a thought. You have to

open your mouth and rebuke it. Start talking to

yourself when no one else is around. Speak

against those devilish thoughts. Entertaining it

makes it gain momentum, but casting it down

exposes it and diminishes it. The devil has

access to your mind, but he can't get in your

behaviors.

Learn to say no. The best way to fight temptation is to *learn to say no when you can say yes so when you have to say no, you can.* You will develop the discipline to say no even when you can say yes. Think about this: when

Learn to say no when you can say yes so when you have to say no, you can.

was the last time you told yourself no? When was the last time you put yourself on a fast; not when your pastor called you to do one, but you did it on your own? When was the last time you vowed to go to the gym, stop eating certain foods, stop watching certain TV shows, and listening to certain music? You have to make the decision to be disciplined, because God will not force you to make those choices. The devil knows what you like and knows the right time and the right way to present it to you to tempt you. Temptation will not magically go away. You have to fight it and say no to it. If you commit to taking it one day at a time, God will help you and it will become easier with every "no."

~ ~ ~

If you are in search of sexual healing and you are divorced, it can be more difficult if you have been used to having sex regularly and have to go back to refraining from it when you now have an appetite for it, even if the intimacy was lost before the divorce happened. The first thing to do is allow yourself time to heal. Allow God to heal your heart. Seek counsel not just from friends, but from a counselor, pastor, or someone else you can trust to ask you questions and tell you when it's the right time to move forward. This way, you won't begin dating prematurely and hurting the new person that you're with. You'll know when you're in a good space by the nature of your temperament. You won't be seeking a new relationship to fill the void of your previous relationship, nor will you project the problems from the old relationship in the new one. Heal first. Date later.

Also, wait until the divorce is final before you begin to date again. Dating while separated still counts as adultery because you are still technically married.

Heal first. Date later.   When you do begin to date, it's important to set boundaries in the relationship so you don't give into temptation. It may seem like a juvenile thing to do, especially since you have already gone through a marriage. You are older and wiser, but temptation will still be a reality. If you set practical boundaries in place (spend time together in public, don't spend the night late at night, etc.), it will be easier to resist.

If you have children with an ex and you begin to date again, think about when you will involve your children in the relationship. Some people involve their children too soon and end up damaging them. Be patient and guard your heart for the sake of you and your kids.

My Prayer for You:

Father I intercede for my generation. I declare today that we give ourselves back to you. We will not be sex-ridden, disease-ridden, and child-ridden. We will not be without morals. We will not be without values. We will not cheat on our spouses, coming to church with our girlfriends and boyfriends while we're still married, sitting and holding hands while still married. The devil is a lie. Satan, the Lord rebukes you. I will not be silent while the world is making millions of dollars talking about sex and perverting the minds of God's people. God, I declare restoration today. I come against the spirit of perversion in the name of Jesus. I shift it. I come against that sexual stronghold; that "can't help it" spirit. I break it.

I pray that You give your people a spirit of discipline. I pray that You give them a supernatural power to overcome. I pray that You don't condemn them, but you convert them in the name of Jesus.

I break that guilty spirit. I break the spirit of condemnation. Whom the Son sets free is free indeed. I declare freedom in the name of Jesus. Every stronghold, I break it today. Every distraction, I break it today. Every act of immorality, I break it today. Every spirit of perversion, I break it today. Every stronghold that the enemy will place over our minds, I break it today. I speak healing from rape,

abuse, and molestation. I call out that

pedophile spirit today. I break that spirit of

pornography. YouTube won't have a hold on

us. The Internet won't have a hold on us. The

blood of Jesus prevails. God, give them power

over the enemy. Give them power over every

work of darkness. Give them power and

deliverance. I break it! I break it in the name of

Jesus.

Reflection:

Who in your family or circle of friends do you trust with your secrets? Will you make the commitment to discuss your secrets with them this week?

_____

_____

_____

When was the last time you denied your body something? If it's been a while, pick something to deny yourself this week. It can be as simple as skipping dessert for a day. It may seem small, but it will help you begin to develop discipline.

_____

_____

_____

If you're single, resisting temptation can be

easier if you keep yourself busy. What are some

things you like to do? Read? Play sports?

Exercise? Make a list of things you like to do

and next time temptations arise, try distracting

yourself with an activity.

_____

_____

_____

_____

Notes:

It's Time to "Tear it Up"

For though we live in the world, we do not wage war as the world does. The weapons we fight with are not the weapons of the world. On the contrary, they have divine power to demolish strongholds. We demolish arguments and every pretension that sets itself up against the knowledge of God, and we take captive every thought to make it obedient to Christ. And we will be ready to punish every act of disobedience, once your obedience is complete. You are judging by appearances. If anyone is confident that they belong to Christ, they should consider again that we belong to Christ just as much as they do.

2 Corinthians 10:3-7

Healing from past sexual sins will be a continuous battle. It's easy to get free, but it's a walk to stay free. Even though we walk and operate in the flesh, our battles are spiritual. Before getting married, to Christ or a person, it is best to deal with the mess of the past so you don't create a crisis. To move forward in a healthy manner, you need to be free from your sexual history. How do you

It's easy to get free, but it's a walk to stay free.

begin to move forward and break soul ties and recover from the pain of your past?

1.) Admit that your sexual identity needs reshaping.

Nothing gets fixed if we deny that it's broken. What is your soul trying to say? Listen to it and let your sexual choices guide you into a greater level of wisdom and self-understanding. It's okay to have soul ties that still need cutting. However, it's not okay to stay there and ignore your need for healing and freedom.

2.) Make your own list.

This will be a painful process, but a complete list of all your sexual encounters will reveal a great deal. For each partner, ask yourself, "Why did I have sex with them?" or "Why was I romantically involved with that person at all?" Work your way down the list one person at a time, making note of your responses.

3.) Identify the theme.

Once your list is made, take an honest look at the big picture. What common themes become evident? What do most of these men or women have in common? What does that tell you?

4.) Learn the lesson.

Based on what you've learned so far, what revelations are you able to receive? Do you recognize what it is that you've really been looking for? What area of neediness have you been trying to satisfy through dysfunctional relationships? How has that worked for you?

5.) Forgive others.

While it's easy to throw a stone at all the people on our list for using or abusing us, we have to recognize that in many instances, we've taught them how to treat us. It takes two to tango, and we play a part in the dance of dysfunction. A healthy person doesn't fall prey to the schemes of an unhealthy person. Ignoring our part and

It takes two to tango and we play a part in the dance of dysfunction.

harboring resentment toward the other person for their part is like *you* drinking poison while hoping the other person dies. This bitterness does you no good. Do yourself a favor. Forgive the people on your list. Declare that they don't owe you anything. Acknowledge that they were most likely in the same boat as you – seeking to medicate their own emotional pain while ignorant to what damage was really being done.

6.) Forgive yourself.

Forgiving everyone else but harboring resentment toward yourself won't fully sever any soul ties. If you truly want to be free, you have to extend forgiveness toward the one

your choices have hurt the most: yourself.

Forgive yourself for being so hungry for

attention and affection. Give yourself what your

heart has been yearning for all along:

unconditional love and acceptance.

7.) Create a "no contact" rule.

The most damaging thing you can do is

go down your list and try to contact any of

those old partners, even if it's for "asking

forgiveness" from them. That makes about as

much sense as an alcoholic returning to all of

his favorite bars to say to the bartender, "I'm

sorry I came in here. I'm not going to drink

anymore." If you're really serious about cutting all soul ties, you'll let go of any need to reconnect with previous partners, regardless of how noble your reasons for wanting to do so may seem. If you have children with any of your past partners, leave conversation with them about the children only.

8.) Create a "no comparison" rule.

Dragging a ton of soul ties and sexual baggage into the bedroom we share with our spouses is incredibly unfair. Before marriage and during marriage, commit to avoiding all comparisons of your spouse to past partners: mentally, emotionally, physically, or spiritually.

Allow your spouse to be the unique individual that he or she is, not the lesser version of someone else.

9.) Keep your slate clean.

> Allow your spouse to be the unique individual that he or she is, not the lesser version of someone else.

Now that you're aware of just how much residue remains after an inappropriate relational encounter, avoid deep emotional connections with any person you aren't married to. Establish firm boundaries in your work and social relationships such that you don't find yourself in the middle of an emotional or sexual affair ever again.

10.) Forget intensity and focus on intimacy.

Maybe these suggestions make you feel as if you are going on an emotional starvation diet. You may be thinking, *Can't I have any fun?* Yes, you can, but not at your own heart's expense, which is ultimately what happens when we create a lot of inappropriate soul ties. I know that such relational rendezvous create a lot of intensity, but intensity doesn't last. Intimacy does. Focus on getting to know your spouse (who is God until you get married) even better than you already do, and knowing yourself better. Invest your energies into spicing up your own love life (with God) rather than trying to create a new one.

Intensity doesn't last. Intimacy does.

11.) Burn it! After you do the work, take the list and burn it, as a symbol of liberty.[1] Don't feel guilty about what you've done. Don't be subject to the things of your past. You may not be where you want to be, but you're not where you used to be.

Keep your slate clean. Once God gets you clean, stay clean. Avoid deep emotional connections with men and women that you're not married to. Establish firm boundaries on all

---

[1] Be careful when burning your list! Exercise all fire safety precautions. We are not liable for any fires that occur as a result of this exercise.

your relationships. Avenge all your disobedience with obedience. As much as you've made bad decisions, keep that same fire as motivation to make good decisions. If you went wild for the devil before, go wild for God now. As bad as you've been and as hard as you went in the world, that's how hard you should now go for God.

You may have experienced and explored your sexuality prematurely, but if you are convicted today, you are alive. God can make you whole and give you freedom from the decisions you made. He will restore you. You can do nothing about your past, but you can make a choice to take it one day at a time and

give your body back to God every day. Ask Him
to restore you. God wants to restore you and
put the pieces back together again and make
you whole. God will give you freedom and
restore your sexual life so you can enjoy it the
way He intended. G-Rated sex is when you
have sex God's way.

My Prayer for You:

I declare strongholds are destroyed today in the name of Jesus. Yokes are broken today in the name of Jesus. There will be no guilt about the past. I pray that the yoke destroying, burden-bearing power of God take effect on the lives of your people so they will not be subject to the stuff that has tried to take their lives. They will not be dragged back in the name of Jesus. The blood of Jesus covers them. I speak life. I speak liberty. They are forgiven today. The forgiveness of God is upon their lives today. Father, let Your power prevail. Father, we trust You. We bless you. We love you. We believe you today in the name of Jesus.

If you believe it, repeat this prayer: Lord forgive me for all of my sins of my past. Wash it in the name of Jesus. I want to never be the same, God. I pray today my day of healing, my day of transformation. God, I pray today that you tear up everything in my life that's not like you. I pray that you would rip it up. I'm not proud of it. Justify my sins. Cover me from my sins. Forgive me of my sins. I want to never be the same today. I desire you more than anything. Let your power and presence rest on me today in the name of Jesus. I declare today, Father, I never want to be the same in Jesus' name. Amen.

Made in the USA
Las Vegas, NV
12 December 2023

82640091R00080